Baseball 101

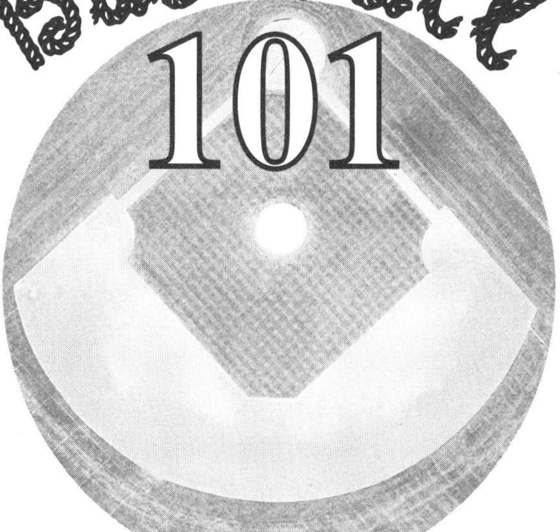

Steven Jay Griffel

Reading Advantage Authors
Laura Robb
James F. Baumann
Carol J. Fuhler
Joan Kindig

Project Manager
Ellen Sternhell

Editor
Jeri Cipriano

Design and Production
Preface, Inc.

Photography
Front cover © Peter Dazeley/Getty Images; pp. 1, 10, back cover © Barrie Rokeach/Getty Images; pp. 7, 16, 49, 55, 58 tc © Bettmann/Corbis; p. 8 © Lee Snider/The Image Works; p. 12 © David Madison; p. 18 © BSF/NewSport/Corbis; pp. 20, 21, 30 © AP Photo; p. 26 © Duomo/Corbis; p. 27 © Nathan Bilow/Getty Images; p. 31 © Elsa/Getty Images; p. 35 © Stephen Dunn/Getty Images; pp. 38, 43, 47, 53, 59, 61 © Reuters/Corbis; p. 40 © V. J. Lovero/Getty Images; p. 45 © Doug Pensinger/Getty Images; p. 58 bc © AP Photo/Eric Draper; p. 62 tl © Rick Stewart/Getty Images; tc © AP Photo/Paul Chiasson; tr © Ezra Shaw/Getty Images; cl © Andy Lyons/Getty Images; c © AP Photo/file; cr, bl © Craig Jones/Getty Images; bc © Scott Halleran/Getty Images; br © Eliot J. Schechter/Getty Images

Trademarks and trade names are shown in this book strictly for illustrative purposes and are the property of their respective owners. The author's references herein should not be regarded as affecting their validity.

Copyright © 2005 by Great Source Education Group, a division of Houghton Mifflin Company. All rights reserved.

No part of this work may be reproduced or transmitted in any form or by any means, electronic or mechanical, including photocopying and recording, or by any information storage or retrieval system without the prior written permission of Great Source Education Group, unless such copying is expressly permitted by federal copyright law. Address inquiries to Permissions, Great Source Education Group, 181 Ballardvale Street, Wilmington, MA 01887.

Great Source® is a registered trademark of Houghton Mifflin Company.

Printed in the United States of America

International Standard Book Number: 0-669-51419-5

3 4 5 6 7 8 9 10 – RRDC – 09 08 07 06 05

CONTENTS

Introduction **Baseball: Our National Pastime**   5

LESSON 1 **It All Starts with Pitching**   9
Pitching Basics
Using Your Head
Throwing a Pitch
The Flamethrowers
The Artists

LESSON 2 **The Sweet Science of Hitting**   24
Tools of the Trade
Getting into the Swing of Things
Keep Your Eye on the Ball
Using the Whole Field

LESSON 3 **Getting on Base**   36
Take a Walk
The Art of Bunting
Getting Hit

LESSON 4 Catch It and Throw It 44
The Backstops
Diamond Dazzles
The Hot Corner
Stopping at First
The Outfielders

LESSON 5 The Big Boppers 54
The Babe
The M & M Boys
McGwire and Sosa
Barry Bonds

LESSON 6 The Stars of the World 60
Japan and Korea
All-American Stars

Glossary 63

INTRODUCTION

Baseball: Our National Pastime

Baseball is a simple game with a lot of rules. Does that sound funny? It makes sense, if you think about it. All you need is a bat, a ball, and a baseball glove, and you can play the game.

People play baseball in all kinds of places. Baseball is played on city streets and playgrounds. It's played in parks and on rocky fields. And it's played in grand stadiums where the field is a perfect, miracle green. Baseball is a game played by young and old and everyone in between.

Because it has been such a popular sport for so many years, baseball has been called our national pastime. People say baseball is as American as apple pie and ice cream. But baseball actually has its origins in an English children's game called rounders.

There were some rich and important Americans who thought baseball should have American roots. They put together a special committee to make sure that baseball was seen as an American sport.

In 1907, the committee named Abner Doubleday as the game's inventor. Doubleday was a Civil War hero. He even became a general. After the war, he became a well-known speaker and writer. But he had nothing to do with baseball. The committee ignored Alexander Joy Cartwright even though he was the one who actually invented the modern baseball field in 1845. And it was Cartwright who wrote the first rules and regulations for the modern game.

In the early years of baseball (second half of the 1800s), Americans of all classes and races began playing the game. The first African Americans to play major league baseball were the Walker brothers, Fleet and Welday. They played for Toledo of the American Association in 1884. But black players gradually began to be excluded from the white leagues.

By the beginning of the new century, there were no black players in organized baseball. But black players continued to play the game. They played on all-black teams. Eventually, they formed their own baseball leagues. But they would not again play alongside white players in the major leagues until 1947. That was the year that Jackie Robinson broke the "color barrier" by joining the Brooklyn Dodgers.

Robinson's rookie season with the Brooklyn Dodgers was in 1947. That year, Robinson was voted National League Rookie of the Year. He had 12 homers, a league-leading 29 steals, and a .297 average. In 1949, he was chosen the league's Most Valuable Player. He also won the batting title that same year with a .342 average. Robinson was elected to the Hall of Fame in 1962, his first year of eligibility.

Today, in Cooperstown, New York, you can visit the National Baseball Hall of Fame. You can see all sorts of exhibits that celebrate the history of baseball. This is a place for the best of the best. Black, white, and all the rest are remembered there for the greatness and joy they brought to the game.

Are you ready for some baseball talk and strategy? Then step up to the plate!

The National Baseball Hall of Fame and Museum was officially opened on June 12, 1939. But the first election of players was held a few years earlier in 1936. The first five players elected were Ty Cobb, Babe Ruth, Honus Wagner, Christy Mathewson, and Walter Johnson. Today, hundreds of thousands of people visit the Hall of Fame each year.

LESSON 1

It All Starts with Pitching

Baseball experts are always saying that pitching is ninety percent of the game. That means that pitching is the single most important part of any baseball game. If a pitcher performs well, there is a very good chance that his or her team will win.

Imagine that you're the pitcher of today's game. You're holding the ball in your glove and standing on the *pitcher's mound*. This is the slightly elevated center of the infield, which is called the *diamond*. Facing you, exactly 60 feet, 6 inches away, is *home plate*. Squatting behind *home plate* is the *catcher*.

Behind you and to your left is *first base*. Directly behind you is *second base*. In front of you and to your right is *third base*. One of your teammates is playing near each of these bases. There is another player on the field, standing between second base and third base. He or she is the shortstop.

This is your *infield*. If your team players are good at catching and throwing, they will help you keep the other team from scoring runs.

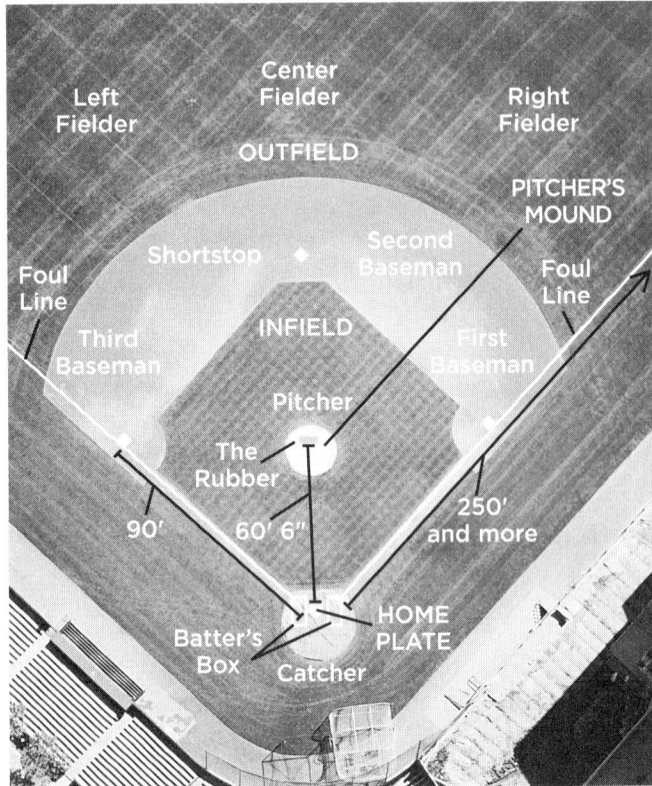

Major league rules say just how far the parts of an infield should be from each other, right down to the inch. But outfields are not as strictly regulated. Some ballparks are bigger than others.

For a moment, you turn your back on home plate and face the *outfield*. There are no bases out there. It's just an open area of neatly mowed grass. On your far left is a white line. It stretches all the way from home plate, past third base, to a wall, a few hundred feet away. A similar line is on your right. It stretches from home plate, past first base, all the way again to the outfield fence.

Three of your teammates are standing in this outfield. They are, from left to right (you see how logical all this is?) the *left fielder, center fielder,* and *right fielder*. This is your *outfield*. If they're good at catching and throwing, they will help you keep the other team from scoring runs. Sound familiar? Hold that thought.

Pitching Basics

You turn around and are once again facing home plate and the catcher. It's time to get going.

Before the actual game starts, you want to loosen up your arm. You begin by throwing some practice pitches to the catcher. You throw the ball gently. After each throw, the catcher tosses the ball right back to you.

You're not thinking baseball right now. You're not even thinking about real pitching. You're just trying to relax. You want to stretch your arm, shoulder, back, and leg muscles. After a few more slow-toss pitches, you gradually throw a few a little harder. Then you throw a few balls out to your catcher. You let rip with a good fastball. *WHUMP!* The ball explodes into the catcher's mitt, or glove, with a heavy thud.

Then you throw a few of your other best pitches. You might throw a few curve balls, pitches that go to the right or left. You might try them at different speeds: a slow curve *(slurve)* or a fast curve. (This is not a *furve,* but a sharp, breaking pitch.)

This is the classic two-seam fastball grip.

Actually, no one under the age of twelve or thirteen should ever experiment with curve balls, sliders, split-fingers, or knuckle balls. These pitches put added pressure and strain on the elbow and are dangerous for young players. If you're young and you want to be a pitcher, develop your arm strength and accuracy by throwing fastballs. But, for now, let's pretend you are an older, experienced pitcher.

The umpire has been watching you. He is the judge or referee who makes official rulings during the game. The umpire has been timing your warm-up. He is actually counting the number of practice pitches you throw. Now he gives you a signal to start the game. "Play ball!" he bellows. His booming voice sounds like a human megaphone.

The first hitter from the other team enters the *batter's box*. It's called a "box," but it's just a rectangular area painted on either side of home plate. The batter must stand inside one of the boxes. A right-handed batter stands to the right of home plate (from the pitcher's point of view). A left-handed batter stands to the left of home plate.

Well, this is the moment of truth. Let the game begin!

Using Your Head

So, what's the first thing you do? Throw a pitch? Is that what you said? Hold on, there! What's your hurry? You must first make some mental preparations. One of the great things about baseball is that there is a lot of time between plays (even between pitches) for both sides to plan strategy. "Half of this game is ninety percent mental," Philadelphia Phillies manager Danny Ozark once remarked.

Well, moving right along. . . What mental preparations are you making? You're not sure? Consider this: each time a pitcher faces a batter is a unique situation. You, as the pitcher, have to know

✓ *What inning is it? (Each team takes turns on offense and defense.)*
✓ *How many outs have been made? (Three outs make one team's half of the inning.)*
✓ *Are there any runners on base?*
✓ *What is the score?*
✓ *Who is the batter?*
✓ *Is he a lefty or a righty?*
✓ *What kinds of pitches does he like to hit?*
✓ *What kinds of pitches give him trouble?*

Once you are sure you know the answers to these questions, you are ready to pitch to a batter. (For your information, there are approximately one billion rules that govern baseball. OK, that's an exaggeration. You can review all the official rules online. Watch out! The rules go on forever!)

Throwing a Pitch

As an experienced pitcher, you know that you have to keep one foot on the *pitcher's rubber* as you deliver each pitch. You look at your catcher. He gives you a signal: one finger for a fastball, two for a curve, three for a changeup. (A *changeup* is a slow pitch intended to throw off the batter's timing.) The catcher also indicates where to throw the pitch: on the inside or outside part of the plate, high or low.

Now you're ready. You take a deep breath. You begin your wind-up. You throw. "Strike one!"

If you throw three strikes without the batter hitting the ball into fair play (between the white lines of the playing field), the batter is out by strikeout. If the batter hits the ball out over the field, one of your eight teammates will try to catch the ball on the fly (before it hits the ground) to make an out.

If a fair ball hits the field, your fielders will try to catch the ball after it has bounced and throw it to a player covering a base to get the runner out.

If the batter does not swing at a pitch you've thrown outside the *strike zone*, the umpire will signal, "Ball!" If you throw four *balls*, the batter gets a *walk*. A walk allows the batter to go to first base. So, from the batter's point of view, a walk is as good as a hit.

Sandy Koufax (Brooklyn and Los Angeles Dodgers, 1955–1965) was a dominant pitcher for five straight seasons. Koufax had an explosive fastball and sharp-breaking curve ball. An arm injury forced Koufax to retire early. For the last five years of his career, Koufax was at his best. Because of that period, many sports writers rate him as the best pitcher of all time.

The FlameThrowers

Perhaps the most exciting kind of pitcher to watch is the flamethrower. This is a person who can rear back and blow a ball right past the batter. This is someone who can throw blazing heat. The ball goes so fast that by the time the batter swings, the ball has exploded into the catcher's mitt.

Nowadays, there are radar guns that can measure the speed of a pitch. In the days before radar guns, Bob Feller (Cleveland Indians, 1936–1956), one of baseball's all-time great pitchers, measured his fastball against a motorcycle going 100 miles per hour. The fastball won.

Bob Gibson (mostly with the St. Louis Cardinals, 1959–1975) used to terrorize batters. He liked to throw hard near the inside part of home plate. If he thought a batter was standing too close to the plate, he'd knock him down. His catcher, Tim McCarver, called Gibson "the luckiest pitcher I ever saw. He always pitches when the other team doesn't score any runs!" Of course, Gibson wasn't lucky; he was just very great.

Pitcher Roger Clemens certainly deserves his nickname "The Rocket." Twice, Clemens struck out 20 batters in a 9-inning game. That's a record. Clemens also won a record 6 Cy Young Awards. The Cy Young Award is given each year to the best pitcher in the league. Clemens also owns some fancy jewelry. He won World Series championship rings with the Yankees in 1999 and 2000.

Maybe the greatest fastball pitcher of all time was Nolan Ryan. He had an amazing 27-year career (1966–1993). During his career, he struck out 5,714 batters! That's more than any other pitcher in major league history. Ryan relied mostly on his near 100-mph fastball. It was nicknamed "The Ryan Express." Ryan ended his career with 324 wins. That includes a record 7 no-hitters.

As a young player, Ryan was hugely talented, but no one was sure he would succeed. It's hard to believe, but 294 players were selected in the baseball draft ahead of him. During his first seven years with the New York Mets, Ryan was sometimes impressive but terribly uneven. But he worked hard and was encouraged by his coaches. Ryan became a great pitcher and was admitted into Baseball's Hall of Fame in 1999.

The great New York Yankee Joe DiMaggio called Leroy "Satchel" Paige "the best and fastest pitcher I've ever faced." Satchel Paige is considered by many to be the greatest pitcher in the history of the Negro Leagues. For 22 years, Paige beat the competition in front of sell-out crowds.

Paige did not get his chance to pitch in the major leagues until 1948. That was one year after Jackie Robinson entered the major leagues. By baseball standards, Paige was an old man. He was almost 50! But the Cleveland Indians were in need of extra pitching for the pennant race. Baseball owner Bill Veeck tested Paige's accuracy before offering him a big-league contract.

As the story is told, Veeck placed a cigarette on the ground to be used as a home plate. Paige took aim at the tiny target. He fired five fastballs. All but one sailed directly over the cigarette. Veeck was indeed pleased, and Paige helped the Indians win the pennant, or championship.

In 1965, Paige took the mound for the last time, throwing three scoreless innings for the Kansas City Athletics. He was believed to be 59 years old. In 1971, Leroy "Satchel" Paige was given the ultimate honor. He was elected to join the very best in the Hall of Fame.

Top part of Satchel Paige's Hall of Fame plaque in Cooperstown

Most of Satchel Paige's great career was spent in the Negro Leagues. Paige estimated that he pitched twenty-five hundred games—and won two thousand—*before* he ever reached the majors. At his peak, during the 1930s, Paige claimed he won sixty games a season and averaged fifteen strikeouts a game. Paige wrote a book about the story of his life. He called the book *Maybe I'll Pitch Forever.*

The Artists

Many major league pitchers are like artists. Because they don't have a blazing fastball to whiz past batters, they have to be more subtle, crafty—more *artistic*. These pitchers rely on their control more than they do on the speed of their pitches. They try to "paint" the corners of the plate. They attempt to hit exact spots with the accuracy of a laser.

These artists throw many different kinds of pitches. Each pitch varies. It depends on how the ball is gripped and the position or angle of the pitcher's arm when he releases the ball. It also depends on how hard the ball is thrown. The cut fastball, the split-finger fastball, the slider, the curve, and the sinker all have unique movements.

The toughest pitch to throw accurately is the knuckle ball. It is perhaps also the toughest pitch to hit. Great knuckle ball pitchers like Hoyt Wilhelm and Phil Niekro were masters. They knew just how to dig their fingernails into the cowhide. They knew how to avoid the seams and to push the ball rather than throw it. The result is an extremely slow pitch. The ball appears to *dance* from side to side. Batters hate it. They say a knuckle ball is like a fluttering butterfly.

Some pitchers secretly alter the surface of the ball to make it behave strangely. Pitchers have been known to scuff a ball and spit on a ball. Pitchers have done all kinds of weird things to change the flight of a ball. But all these things are illegal. They also violate the idea of fair play. Even so, they seem to have always been part of baseball.

Los Angeles Dodgers pitcher Don Sutton (1966–1988) was often accused of using a foreign substance on the ball to make it move in ways to fool batters. "Not true at all," Sutton once replied. "Vaseline is manufactured right here in the United States!"

LESSON 2

The Sweet Science of Hitting

You've shown you've got what it takes on the pitcher's mound. But how are you with a bat in your hands? Pitching may be an art, but hitting has been called a science.

Now, you might say, "Science! You call hitting a ball with a bat science? Ridiculous!"

Tools of the Trade

Hold on, now. No one said baseball was rocket science. But hitting a baseball does have a lot to do with physics. Take a look at the facts.

To begin, let's start with the baseball itself. It's not very big. The rules say it must be $9\frac{1}{4}$ inches around and weigh $5\frac{1}{4}$ ounces. How big is that? Well, it really depends on how the batter sees the ball. If you're a batter and the pitched ball is traveling 100 miles per hour, the ball may *seem* no larger than a pea. But if the ball is thrown slowly, it might *appear* as large as a grapefruit. So, practically speaking, the size of the ball depends on the batter's view of it.

Unlike the legal size of the ball, the size of the bat is not always the same. Major League rules say that the bat must be a smooth, round stick made out of one piece of solid wood. The bat cannot be more than $2\frac{3}{4}$ inches at its thickest part. And it cannot be more than 42 inches in length.

Some very strong batters like to use the longest, heaviest bats. They feel that the bigger the bat, the more power they will have. (The biggest bat is not as big as a caveman's club, but you get the picture.) Of course, it's not easy to swing the largest bat. So, if you're not a very powerful batter, or if the pitcher is throwing very hard, you might want to use a lighter bat. In fact, many batters use different-sized bats. They choose a bat depending on what kind of pitcher they are facing.

Little League, school, and college baseball players usually use aluminum bats. Aluminum bats last longer than wooden bats, which makes them cheaper to use. These bats are lighter and can be swung faster. Some people say that a ball bounces off an aluminum bat as if off a trampoline. The ball seems to travel faster and farther.

Professional baseball leagues do not allow aluminum bats. They want to protect their historical records. And they want the players' performance to be the result of human ability, not technology.

Now that we have discussed the tools of the trade, let's get back to the science of hitting.

A Chicago Cubs slugger from 1992–2004, Sammy Sosa was born in the Dominican Republic. Sosa didn't pick up a real bat until he was 14. But he was so good he signed a minor league contract when he was only 16! Sosa became a great major league home-run hitter. He was the first Latino ever to hit 500 career home runs.

Getting into the Swing of Things

After getting into the batter's box, the first thing a batter must do is grip the bat the right way. For a right-handed batter, the right hand goes on top. For lefties, the left hand goes on top. The bat should rest in the middle of the fingers, not in the palm of the hands.

Next, a batter must have a comfortable stance. Usually, the feet are spread about shoulder-width apart. Balance is the key. Batters should keep their weight on the balls of their feet.

This is a right-handed batter's grip. Note how the hands are touching.

Can you guess what comes next? Yes, it's the swing! When the batter sees the pitch, he tightens his grip. Right before the pitch arrives, he draws back the bat. As he does this, he uses his hips to shift his weight to his back leg. And then, in the split second before the pitch arrives, he shifts his weight forward, stepping toward the ball. His hands come forward. His body twists, swinging the bat. *WHAM!*

You see, it is all a matter of physics. Hitting a baseball involves speed, weight, balance, and torque (a turning or twisting force). It is very scientific.

Ted Williams was a great Boston Red Sox slugger. He even wrote a book called *The Science of Hitting,* which generations of hitters have studied.

Along with Babe Ruth, Williams is considered by many experts to be the greatest hitter who ever lived. Some great hitters had better batting averages. Other batters hit more home runs. But in terms of hitting averages and power, both Ruth and Williams could hit better than any other players who ever played.

It is said that Williams was born to hit a baseball. That sounds a little far-fetched. But it is true that he carried a bat from class to class in school. He was always ready to play baseball.

Keep Your Eye on the Ball

It is also said that Williams had super-powerful eyesight. Some people say he could read the label on a baseball as the pitch was coming toward him!

Once he was asked if it was true that he could see the ball as it hit the bat. "Heck, no!" Williams replied. "And I couldn't see the seams. But in the last twenty feet, I could see which way it was spinning." Even that is pretty incredible.

Consider this: if you're a terrific hitter, your batting average will be around .300. That means you get only 3 hits for every ten *at bats* you get. So, even if you're terrific, you are making an out 7 times out of ten!

What makes hitting so difficult? According to the great hitters, making contact with a small, round object that is moving fast is very hard to do. That's the reason baseball is a hard game to play. It is the one major thing that all young players have difficulty doing.

Now here's a way for a star to exit the stage. In his very last time at bat, on September 28, 1960, Ted Williams hit another home run. It was number 521 of his Hall-of-Fame career.

St. Louis Cardinals outfielder Albert Pujols is destined for greatness. In 2003, at the age of only 23, he was named Player of the Year by *The Sporting News*. Pujols became the first player ever to hit 30 home runs, bat .300, and both score and drive in 100 runs in each of his first three seasons.

Using the Whole Field

You now know the importance of standing correctly in the batter's box. You also know that a batter must keep his eye on the ball. But there are other things you'll want to keep in mind if you want to be a top-notch hitter.

One of Ted Williams's basic hitting tips was to tell batters, "Hit your pitch." Can you guess what this means? It means almost every batter hits some pitches better than he hits others. One batter will usually crush a high and inside fastball. Another batter will usually hit the same pitch weakly or miss it altogether. A good hitter will try to swing only at pitches he thinks he can hit well.

Of course, a batter doesn't know for sure what kind of pitch will be thrown. Even so, a batter can make an educated guess.

Let's take a look at a batting situation.

You are in the batter's box. The score is tied 1–1. You are the first batter up in the second inning. No runner is on base, and there are no outs.

On the mound is a blazing fastball pitcher. You know he can consistently throw his fastball for strikes. He also has a big curve ball. But it's not nearly as accurate. You know he has more confidence in his fastball. The pitcher also has an off-speed pitch. Every once in a while, you know he'll throw this slow pitch in the hopes of throwing off the timing of your swing.

Of course, as a hitter, you have your own strengths and weaknesses. Curve balls give you trouble. You are good at driving fastballs, but only when they are thrown down the center of the plate or toward the outside of the plate. You hate inside fastballs. When the ball is too close to your body, you can't get your arms fully extended. When you swing at an inside fastball, you sometimes feel like you have the short arms of an alligator.

Some hitters don't like to swing at the pitcher's first pitch. They first like to see what the pitcher's motion is like. In any case, it's hard to guess what a pitcher's first pitch will be.

Remember, it takes four balls to walk a batter. If an umpire calls a ball on the first pitch, it's not a big deal. So a pitcher might try to throw almost any kind of first pitch. On the other hand, if a pitcher thinks a batter won't be swinging, he might take a chance and throw a strike right down the middle of the plate.

If a pitcher throws several balls in a row, he will probably want to throw a different kind of pitch. Or, he might want to throw the same pitch in a different location.

There's a lot to think about! But some hitters rely more on instinct and reflexes than thinking. "How can you hit and think at the same time?" asked New York Yankee catcher Yogi Berra.

Hitting Tips

- ✓ Keep your eye on the ball.
- ✓ Don't over-swing. (Meaning: don't try *too* hard to hit a home run.)
- ✓ Use the whole field. (Meaning: don't try to hit the ball to a certain part of the field. Just try to hit the ball hard wherever it is pitched.)

One of the very best hitters was Stan Musial. Stan "The Man" batted over .300 seventeen times. At one time, Musial held nearly every National League career batting record. His career batting average was a lofty .331. Musial was inducted into Baseball's Hall of Fame in 1969.

Like Musial, Tony Gwynn was a genius with a bat in his hands. He hit over .350 for five consecutive years. Gwynn is tied with Honus Wagner for the most National League batting championships (eight).

Gwynn had one of the more efficient swings in baseball. There was no wasted movement. He hit lefties and righties to all fields and was nearly impossible to strike out. Tony Gwynn was a hitting machine!

LESSON 3

Getting on Base

Imagine that your team has not scored any runs in a long time. It's your turn at bat. No one is on base. As you settle into the batter's box, your coach yells out, "Just get on base!"

Of course, you know that the very best thing you could do would be to hit a home run. Then, you would run around the bases, first to second to third, and touch home plate. Your team would score a run. If you hit a single, you would get to first base. A double would bring you to second base. And a triple would send you all the way to third base.

But there are other ways a batter can get to first base. The luckiest way is if a fielder makes an error. This happens when the batter hits a ball that should result in an out. But players make mistakes. (Hey, even major-leaguers are human!) A fielder might drop the ball or make a bad throw. So, it's called an error, not a hit, and the batter can still get on base.

Take a Walk

Another way for a batter to get to first base is to get a walk. A walk is also called a "base on balls." A walk occurs when a pitcher throws four balls to a batter. (A ball—as opposed to a strike—is a pitch outside the *strike zone*.) The batter is then allowed to go to first base, and thus becomes a base runner.

Usually, a pitcher throws a ball because he lacks perfect control. No one can throw the ball exactly where he wants all the time. But sometimes a pitcher throws a ball because he *doesn't want* to throw a strike.

Why wouldn't a pitcher want to throw a strike? Well, what if the batter was really "hot"? What if he was "sizzling"—hitting the ball hard and with power every time and making it go up high. If you're a smart pitcher, you might not want to throw strikes to this guy. If you threw a pitch in the strike zone, the batter might whack it for a hit! So, you might be better off throwing balls and walking the batter. That might be better than having the batter launch the ball over the wall.

Barry Bonds is one of the very greatest players of all time. In 2001, he set a new season record for home runs by knocking 73 out of the park! In 2002, Bonds continued his super-hot hitting. Many pitchers simply did not want to pitch to him. Instead, they would walk him. They would throw four balls in a row to the catcher—who would be standing far away from home plate!

In 2002, Bonds set a new major league record for walks: 198. In some years, a hundred walks can lead the league. Nearly 200 walks in a single season is out of this world! It's the all-time record.

The Art of Bunting

Another way for a batter to get on base is to bunt. A *bunt* is a kind of swing, very loosely speaking. When bunting, the batter slides his bottom hand down to the knob of the bat. He places his top hand about halfway up the thickest part of the bat. His fingers sort of pinch the part of the bat that faces away from the pitcher. In a sense, the batter attempts to "catch" the ball with the bat.

The idea of bunting is to soak up all the pitch's energy with a soft thud. This will cause the ball to dribble away from the plate, away from the catcher and into the infield. A good bunt creates a good chance. It forces the infielders to field a slowly rolling ball very quickly and to throw it to first base before the batter gets there. Quite often, a bunt forces mistakes. And when that happens, the batter gets to first base.

Some of the greatest bunters in baseball history include Ty Cobb, Phil Rizzuto, Rod Carew, and Brett Butler. Carew, like Cobb, was one of baseball's all-time, great hitters. When bunting, it always looked as if Carew caught the ball with his bat and then dribbled it to whatever part of the field had no one standing in it.

Carew would get ten or more bunt hits every year. That might not sound like many. But they added twenty or more points to his batting average. Brett Butler once got more than thirty bunt hits in a season!

Notice that for bunting, Carew has turned around to face the pitcher.

Getting Hit

There is yet another way for a batter to get to first base. But it can be a very painful lesson to learn. If a pitched ball hits a batter, the batter goes to first base. The rule says a batter must try to get out of the way. But that's not so easy. A pitch thrown at 95 miles per hour takes less than half a second to cross the plate. That doesn't give the batter much time to react.

If the ball hits any part of the batter, the batter gets a free trip to first base. But a free trip to first base can be a costly experience. In one case, it cost a player his life.

In 1920, New York Yankees pitcher Carl Mays hit Cleveland Indians shortstop Ray Chapman in the head with a fastball. Chapman crumpled to the ground. He lay there a long while. Finally, he woke up and was helped out of the batter's box. But on the way to the centerfield clubhouse, he collapsed. He never again woke up. Chapman died the following day.

In most cases, a pitcher will not hit a batter on purpose. If he does hit a batter, he is usually very sorry.

After a pitcher has hit a batter, the pitcher may say something to excuse what he has done. A pitcher usually says one of the three following things:

"The ball slipped."

"It got away from me."

"It was an accident."

Of course, these are the same things a pitcher usually says even if he has hit a batter on purpose. Yes, it does happen. A pitcher will sometimes hit a batter on purpose. If you are innocent and good-hearted, you might ask, "Why would anyone do that?" Well, there are several reasons.

Some batters like to get real close to home plate. They feel they can reach balls pitched near the outside part of the plate more easily. Of course, pitchers don't like batters who crowd, or stand too close to, the plate. They feel it gives the batter an advantage.

Now, it won't work for the pitcher to say to the batter, "Excuse me. But would you please move away from the plate? You are making me uncomfortable." Nah, that's not how it works.

What a pitcher will do is bust a pitch inside on the batter. It's called a "purpose pitch." The purpose is to send a message to the batter: *move back or else!*

Sometimes, if a batter is hit, he will expect his pitcher to hit someone on the other team! Well, you could see how this could get out of hand. Clearly, two wrongs do not make a right.

No one should ever throw a baseball at another player. But accidents—and anger—are part of the game. Beginning in the 1970s, major league players were required to wear protective batting helmets.

LESSON 4

Catch It and Throw It

You have learned a lot about pitching and hitting. But the best pitcher in the world can't win unless his teammates are really good at catching and throwing the ball.

The Backstops

It's probably a good idea to talk about the catcher position first. After all, if there is no catcher, who will throw the ball back to the pitcher? It would take a long time to finish a game without a catcher!

But there's a lot more to being a catcher than just catching the ball and tossing it back to the pitcher. For one thing, a catcher must "call" a good game. A catcher is like a coach on the field. A catcher signals to the pitcher what kind of pitch to throw and where to throw it. A catcher must be good at holding his glove just where he wants the pitch to land. This is called "framing" the pitch. A catcher must also be good at fielding bunts and pop-ups around home plate.

It's also important for a catcher to have a strong arm. When a pitcher goes into his wind-up before throwing a pitch, a base runner may try to run ahead and "steal" the next base. The catcher will try to throw the ball to the fielder before the base runner arrives. If the throw is strong and accurate, the fielder may be able to tag the runner out.

Ivan "Pudge" Rodriguez is one of the best defensive catchers in baseball. All of his catching skills make him very valuable to his team. In fact, he was named Most Valuable Player of the 2003 Florida Marlins World Series championship team.

Diamond Dazzles

It is often said that pitching and defense win games. This is because hitting is an up and down thing. Batters get hot and batters get cold. An entire team might go into a long hitting slump and have a hard time scoring runs. A team can generally play good defense more often than offense. And any team that keeps the other team from scoring many runs has a good chance of winning.

In a typical baseball game, most outs are made by the infielders. Usually, it is the shortstop or the second baseman who makes most of the outs in a game. This is because more balls are hit to the middle of the field than sharply down either side.

Other than the pitcher or the catcher, the shortstop is the most important infielder. On most teams, it is the shortstop who has the best hands. The player with the best hands is the one who is best at fielding, or catching, the ball.

Can you guess why the shortstop is even more important than the second baseman? Take another look at the diagram of the baseball field on page 10.

There are two main reasons why shortstop is the most important infield position. For one thing, it is on the left side of the field. Most batters, just like most human beings, are right-handed. When a right-handed batter hits the ball, he usually pulls it to the left side of the field. So the shortstop usually gets more chances to catch the ball than any other position.

All baseball fans know shortstop Alex Rodriguez by his nickname: A-Rod. Before A-Rod was even 25 years old, many people were calling him the best, all-around shortstop who ever played.

Also, the shortstop plays farther away from first base than the third baseman or second baseman does. On the diagram, it may look like the third baseman is farther away than the shortstop. But the third baseman usually plays much closer to the base, or "bag." The shortstop often plays deep in the hole. That means he plays farther away from the infield, toward left field. The deeper in the hole a shortstop can go, the more balls he can catch. Of course, a shortstop must have a very strong arm to throw to first base from that far away!

Both the shortstop and second baseman must be able to make a strong pivot throw. The pivot throw is used to complete a *double play.* Here's a typical double-play situation:

A runner is on first base. There is one out or no one out. A ground ball is hit to the second baseman. He catches the ball and throws it to the shortstop. The shortstop steps on second base, then pivots, or changes direction, and throws the ball to the first baseman. If the ball is caught before the batter has crossed first base, it's a double play. Two outs were made on one play!

The Hot Corner

Third base is the *hot* corner! When a right-handed hitter pulls a ball right down the line, it's the third baseman's job to make the play. Sometimes a third baseman plays even closer to home plate than usual. He may be expecting the batter to bunt the ball. Or he may be expecting a play at the plate and he wants to be able to throw to the catcher very quickly.

As a fielder, Baltimore Oriole third baseman Brooks Robinson was in a class by himself. Because he caught every ball hit his way, people called him "the human vacuum cleaner." Robinson won the Gold Glove Award for third baseman for sixteen consecutive years!

Sometimes the third baseman may be no more than 50 feet away from the batter. That's almost close enough to shake hands. Not quite, but you get the point. What happens if the batter rockets a ball right at the third baseman when he's standing so close? Well, that's why they call it the hot corner!

Stopping at First

It may not be as hot as third base, but first base is also a very important position. For one thing, a first baseman is involved in more plays than any other player. Every time a ground ball is hit, the first baseman has to hustle to the base and expect a throw from a teammate. Sometimes the throws are high or off-line. That's why most first basemen are tall and have long arms. They have to be able to reach and catch these bad throws.

Sometimes the throws bounce before they reach the first baseman. That's why a first baseman also has to have good hands. However, because he doesn't have to cover as much ground as the other players, a first baseman does not have to be very fast.

The Outfielders

Outfielders on a baseball team are its last line of defense. If a ball gets by an outfielder, a runner has a chance to turn a hit into a double or triple. It's even possible for a runner to fly around all the bases and score on a hit that stays inside the park. That's called an "inside-the-park" home run. But it doesn't happen very often.

Speed

Unlike most infield positions, an outfielder has a lot of ground to cover. That's why most outfielders have good speed.

Playing Smart

An outfielder must always know the situation. How many outs are there? Are there any runners on the bases? What's the score?

Let's say the score is tied. It's the bottom of the ninth inning, or near the end. A runner is on second base. A ground ball gets through the infield for a hit. The runner on second is trying to score. Because the outfielder knows that the runner represents the possible winning run, he will make a throw to try to get the runner out at the plate.

A good outfielder is also aware of weather conditions. Is it a windy day? Which way is the wind blowing? Is the grass wet? (If so, it will slow down a bouncing ball hit to the outfield.)

Smooth Glove

The more confident an outfielder is, the more shallow (closer to the infield) he can play. By playing shallow, an outfielder can prevent a lot of weak fly balls from dropping in for base hits. But an outfielder had better be able to run back and catch a ball hit over his head!

Cannon Arm

An outfielder should have a strong and accurate throwing arm. A strong arm will prevent runners from taking an extra base on a hit or error. An outfielder must also know *where* to throw the ball. The score and the inning tell the outfielder which base to throw to. Sometimes, if an outfielder catches the ball deep in the outfield, he will throw to a "cut-off" man. A "cut-off" man is an infielder who catches the ball from the outfielder and then decides whether to throw it to another base or to hold it.

Like Hall-of-Famers Joe DiMaggio and Willie Mays, Atlanta Braves player Andruw Jones is another great center fielder. Not only does Jones win a Gold Glove almost every year, but he's also a terrific hitter. At the age of 19, Jones hit two home runs in a World Series game.

LESSON 5

The Big Boppers

Is there anything in baseball more exciting than a huge home run? The sound of the bat striking the ball is like a crack of thunder. The ball streaking across the sky looks like a tiny, white comet. Everything becomes still as the ball arches over the wall. Then the fans leap and cheer wildly!

The Babe

No home run hitter dominated the game as Babe Ruth did. Ruth's home run blasts were longer, higher, and harder than anyone had ever seen. And he hit more home runs than anyone at the time thought possible. In 1920, Ruth crushed a record total of 54 home runs. The runner-up was George Sisler with 19. That year Ruth hit more home runs than every major league team except the Phillies (64 home runs)!

Ruth kept on breaking his own records. In 1921, he hit 59 home runs. In 1927, Ruth hit 60 home runs! People thought that record might never be broken.

Babe Ruth began his career in 1914 with the Boston Red Sox. Right away, he was a great hitter *and* a great pitcher! But Red Sox owner Harry Frazee needed money. In 1920, Frazee traded Ruth to the New York Yankees for cash. Bad move! Ruth would lead the Yankees into the World Series seven times. The Red Sox did not win another Series until 2004. Many Red Sox fans believed they were under an 86-year curse for having traded Ruth.

Babe Ruth's record of 60 home runs withstood many challenges. Jimmie Foxx, Hank Greenberg, Ralph Kiner, and a few other great hitters came close. But none of them could equal the Babe's record. That would change, finally, in 1961.

The M & M Boys

That summer, Mickey Mantle and Roger Maris put on a great home run show. On August 13, the two New York Yankees were tied at 45 home runs. Many fans were rooting for Mantle to break the record. He was more popular than Maris. But Mantle got cold and Maris stayed hot. And then Mantle got hurt. It was all up to Roger Maris. The whole country was watching.

Maris hit his 56th home run on September 9. With each passing day, the pressure increased. Reporters and photographers hounded Maris. Maris started losing his temper. He even started losing his hair! On September 26, Maris hit his 60th home run. He tied Babe Ruth! But could he break the record?

October 1 was the last game of the season. That day Maris pulled a fastball from Boston's Tracy Stallard into the right field stands of Yankee Stadium. It was number 61! Maris was the new home run king!

McGwire and Sosa

Maris's record lasted many years. Again, some people thought it would never be broken.

But on September 8, 1998, Mark McGwire hit his 62nd home run of the season. The St. Louis Cardinals slugger hugged his teammates. He hugged Chicago Cubs slugger Sammy Sosa, who competed with McGwire for the home run record. He even embraced five of Roger Maris's children. They were at the game to watch their father's record fall.

All summer, McGwire and Sosa battled for the home run crown. Fans marveled at the explosive power of each player. And they marveled at their sportsmanship. During the pressure-packed home run race, both players showed so much joy and dignity. The two men were making their own legends.

The home run race continued through the final weeks of the season. But McGwire finally pulled away. And he did it in dramatic style. In the Cardinals's final series of the year, McGwire crushed five home runs. There was a new name in the record book: McGwire—70 home runs in a single season.

In 1961, Roger Maris (61 home runs) and Mickey Mantle (54) hit more home runs than any other two players in a single season (top). In 1998, Sammy Sosa (66) and Mark McGwire (70) smashed that record (bottom)!

Barry Bonds

You might say that Barry Bonds was destined for baseball greatness. His father, Bobby Bonds, was a swift and powerful outfielder. His godfather was Willie Mays, one of the greatest players ever. Barry Bonds certainly fulfilled his destiny. In 2001, Bonds hit an astounding 73 home runs.

After the 2004 season with the San Francisco Giants, Bonds had a career total of 703 home runs. And he's still going strong! Bonds has a good chance of breaking the all-time record of 755, held by Hank Aaron.

LESSON 6

The Stars of the World

Baseball's appeal has spread around the world. By 2003, major and minor league players in the United States came from 31 countries. More than 25 percent of all major league players were born outside of the United States.

Many are from Cuba, Mexico, and Puerto Rico. More than half the Latino players come from the Dominican Republic.

Latino Stars:

Livan Hernandez	Cuba
Rafael Furcal	Dominican Republic
Pedro Martinez	Dominican Republic
Vladimir Guerrero	Dominican Republic
Albert Pujols	Dominican Republic
Alfonso Soriano	Dominican Republic
Miguel Tejada	Dominican Republic
Esteban Loaiza	Mexico
Carlos Beltran	Puerto Rico
Javy Lopez	Puerto Rico

Japan and Korea

More and more players are also coming to the Major Leagues from Asia. Hideo Nomo was the first player from Japan to become National League Rookie of the Year (1995). In 2000, Kazuhiro Sasaki won the American League award.

A number of players from Korea have also had great success in the big leagues. These include Hee Seop Choi, Chan Ho Park, and Jae Wong Seo.

Ichiro Suzuki is one of the best baseball players in the world. The Japanese outfielder joined the Seattle Mariners in 2001. That year, Suzuki won the American League Most Valuable Player award and the American League Rookie of the Year award.

All-American Stars

Baseball also boasts many fine young players born right here in the good old USA. Which of them will be truly great? Only time will tell. But if a player does have a truly great career, he just might find himself someday in the Hall of Fame.

Hank Blalock	Adam Dunn	Torii Hunter
Nick Johnson	Andruw Jones	A. J. Pierzynski
Jimmy Rollins	Vernon Wells	Dontrelle Williams

Glossary

at bat taking one's turn to bat

ball a pitch that does not enter the strike zone and is not struck at by the batter

base on balls See **walk.**

batter's box the rectangular areas on either side of home plate in which players stand when batting

bunt a partial swing to gently hit the ball into the infield in an attempt to outrun a throw to first base or advance a base runner

the count the number of balls and strikes against a batter

defense (or **defensive**) the team, or any player of the team, in the field

diamond another name for the infield; it comes from the diamond shape formed by the three bases and home plate

double play when the fielding team gets two base runners out on a hit ball

error a mistake made by a fielder who drops the ball or makes a bad throw

inning that portion of a game within which the teams take turns on offense and defense and in which there are three outs for each team

no hitter a complete game in which the winning pitcher does not give up any base hits

pitcher's mound the elevated dirt area in the center of the diamond from where the pitcher throws to batters

run the score made by an offensive player who touches first, second, third, and home bases in that order

run batted in (or **RBI**) A batter gets an RBI when a base runner crosses the plate as a result of the batter's turn at bat.

signals the hand and arm gestures used by players and coaches to communicate plays with each other

stolen base the result of a runner sprinting to the next base during a pitch

strike zone the pitching target over home plate; it is the area between a batting player's shoulders and knees

walk (or **base on balls**) a batter's free trip to first base, which results from being pitched four balls in his turn at bat